Piano • Vocal • Guitar

Footloose

MUSIC FROM THE MOTION PICTURE

T0056510

ISBN 978-1-4234-2015-2

HAL•LEONARD®
CORPORATION

7777 W. BLUEMOUND RD. P.O. BOX 13819 MILWAUKEE, WI 53213

Visit Hal Leonard Online at
www.halleonard.com

FOOTLOOSE

Words by DEAN PITCHFORD
Music by KENNY LOGGINS

Moderately fast

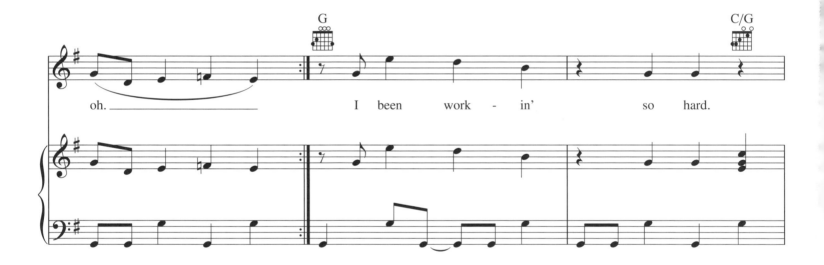

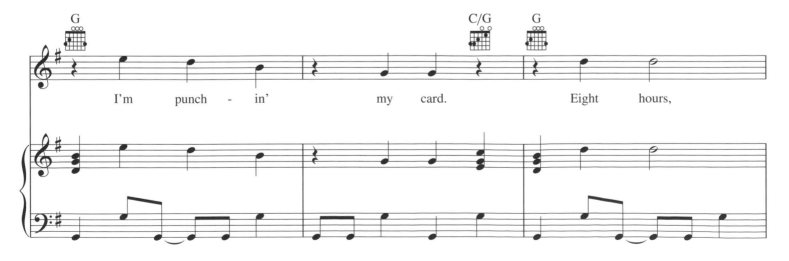

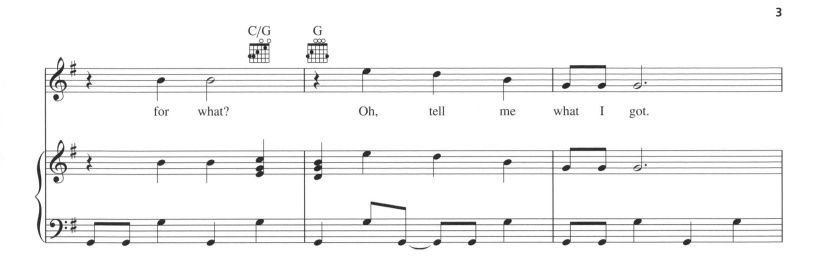

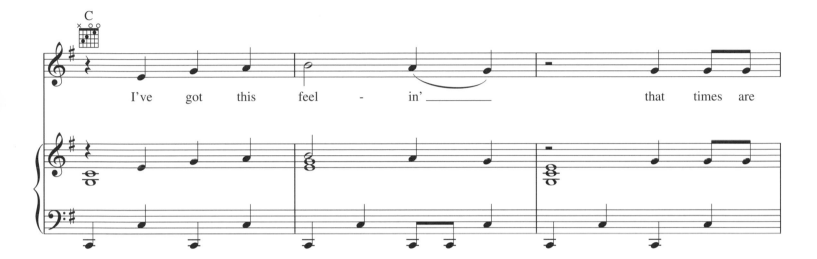

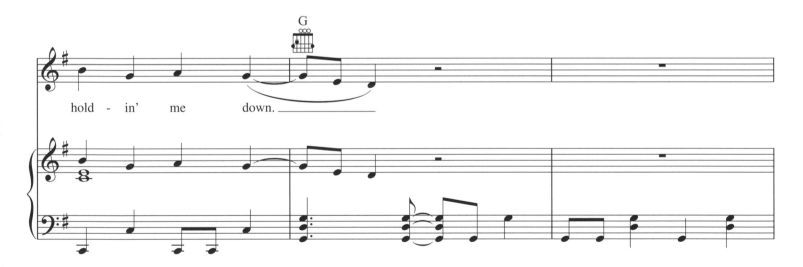

ceil - in' _____ or else I'll tear up this town. ___

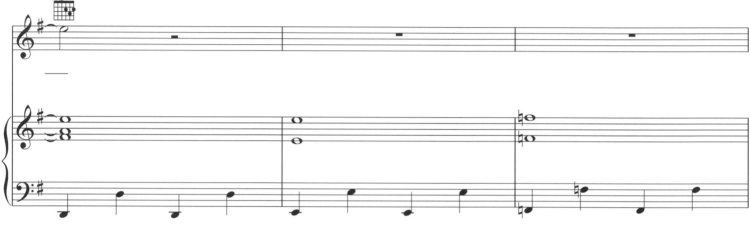

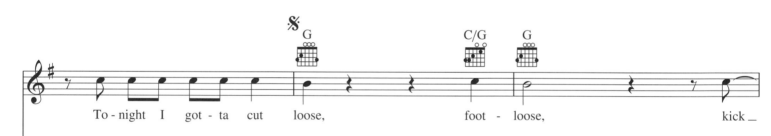

To - night I got - ta cut loose, foot - loose, kick __

__ off your Sun - day shoes. Please, Lou -

Oo wee, Ma -

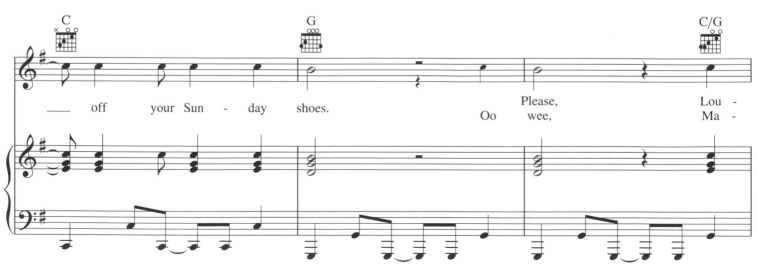

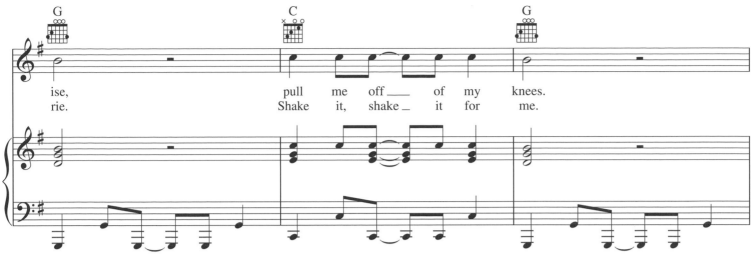

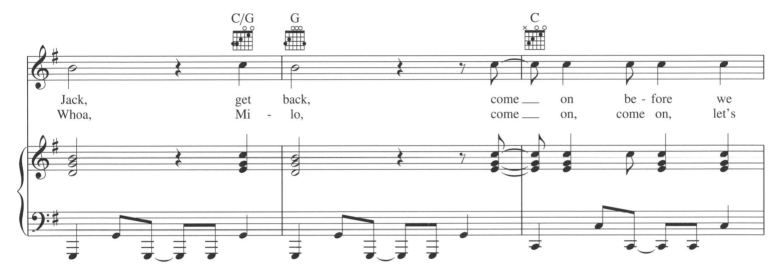

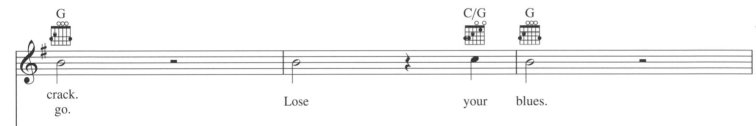

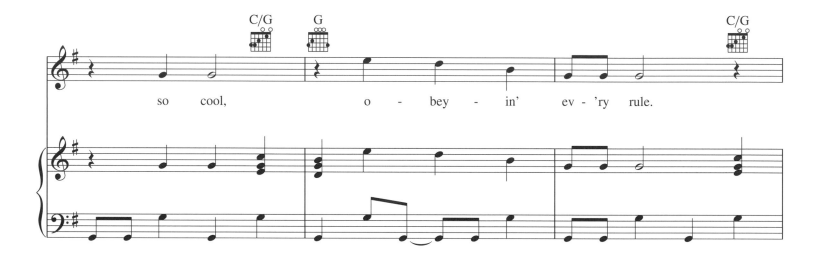

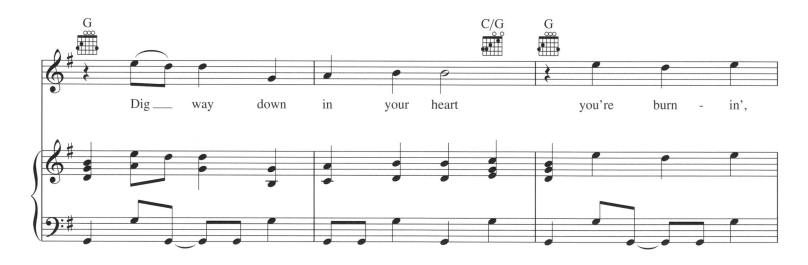

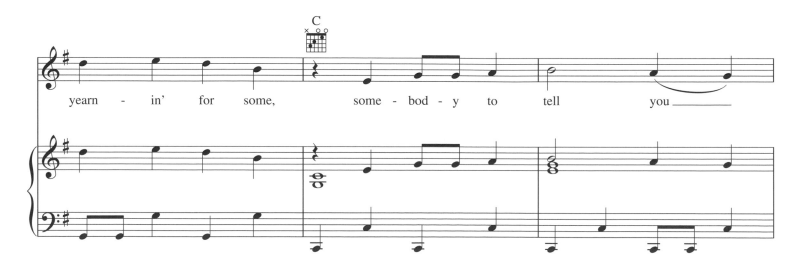

that life ain't a pass - in' you by. _____

I'm try'n' to tell you _____

it will if you don't e - ven try. _____

D.S. al Coda

N.C.

You can fly _____ if you on - ly cut

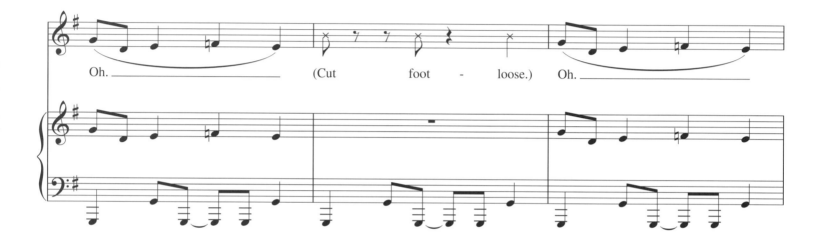

Now I'll take a hold of your soul.

I'm turn-in' it loose. Foot-

loose. Kick ___ off your Sun - day shoes.

Please, Lou - ise, pull me off ___ of my

knees. Jack, get back, come ___

___ on be - fore we crack. Lose your

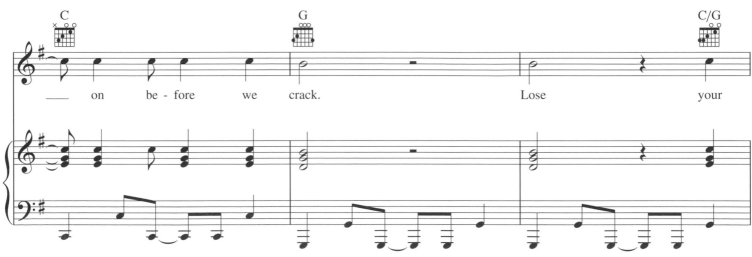

WHERE THE RIVER GOES

Words and Music by ANNE PREVEN,
DREW PEARSON, ZAC BROWN
and WYATT DURRETTE

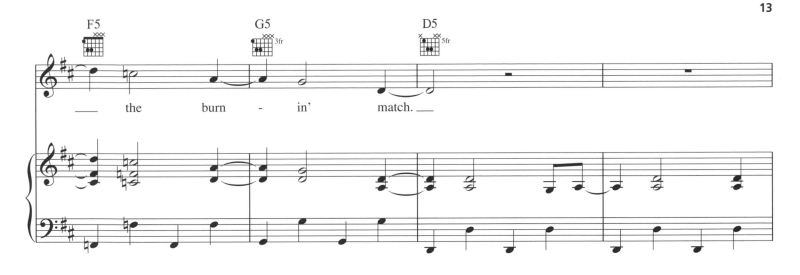

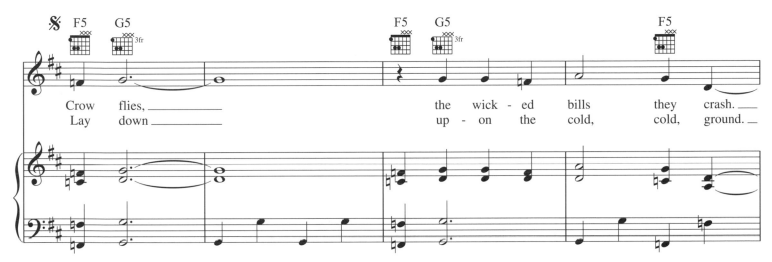

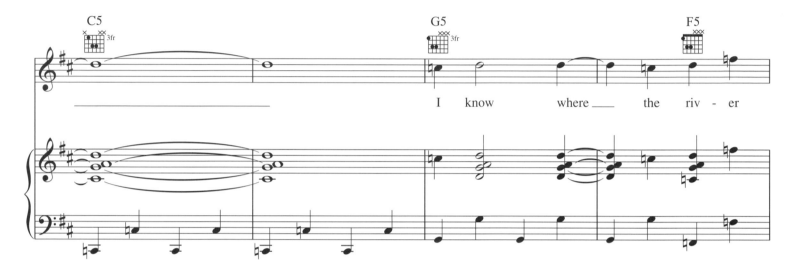

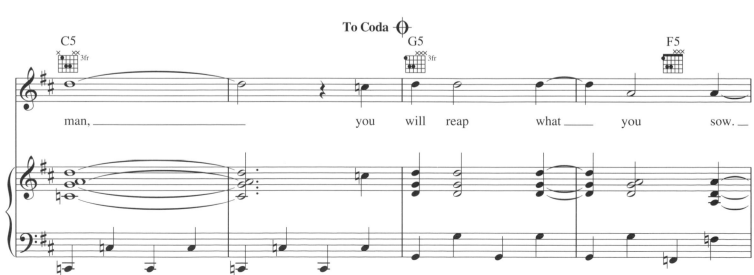

find a way __ to take __ your heart and make it fly a - way, __ so you can

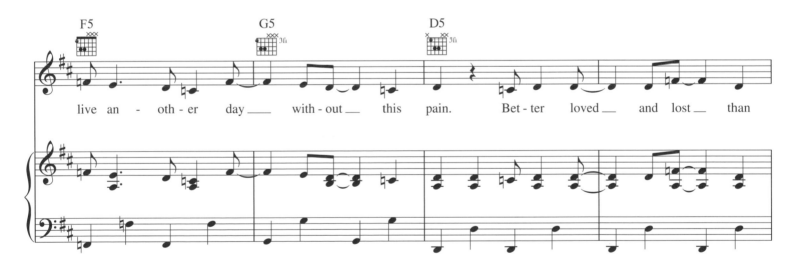

live an - oth - er day __ with - out __ this pain. Bet - ter loved __ and lost __ than

nev - er loved at all. __ That's what they say a black heart is gon - na

D.S. al Coda

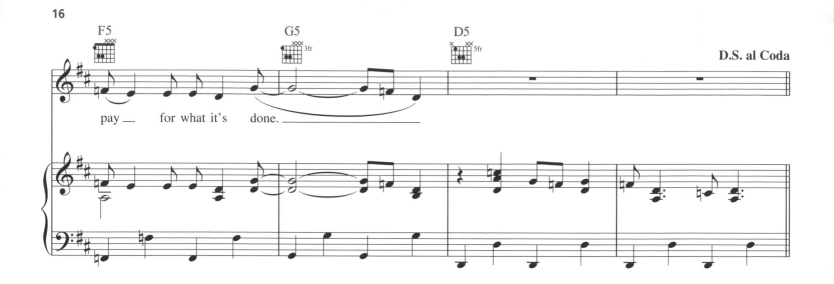

pay __ for what it's done. _____

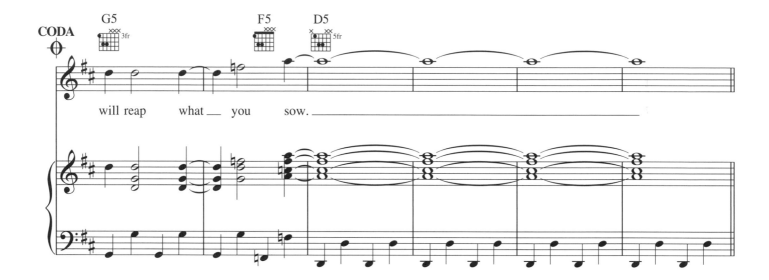

CODA

will reap what __ you sow. _____

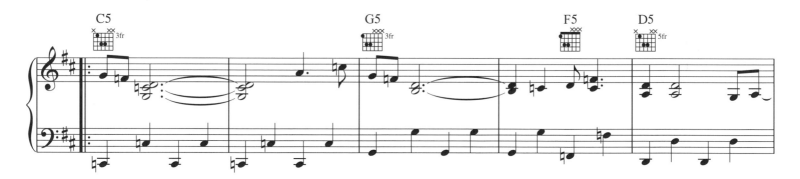

Hey man, _____

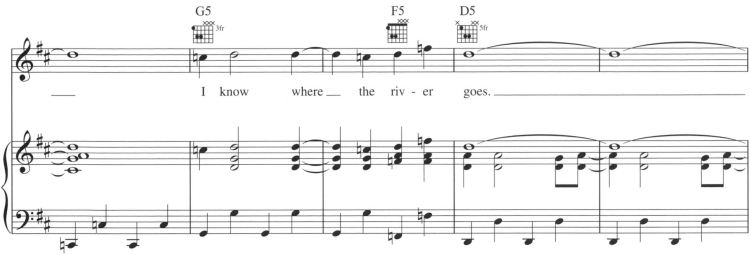

I know where ___ the riv - er goes. _____

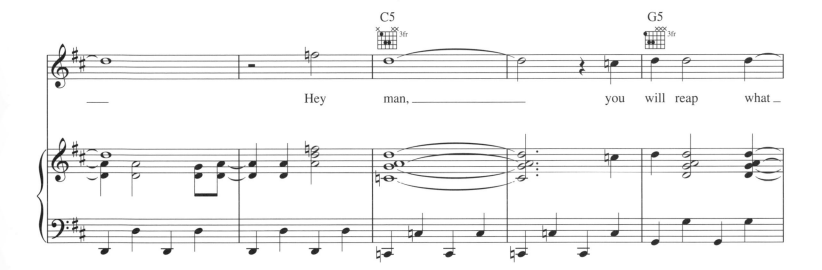

Hey man, _____ you will reap what ___

___ you sow. _____

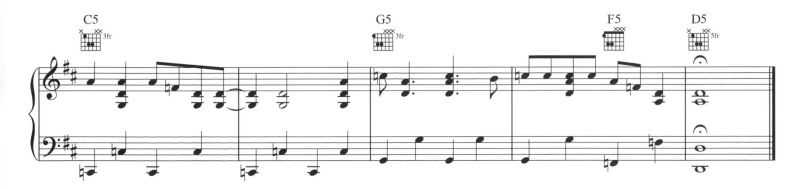

LITTLE LOVIN'

Words and Music by ELISABETH MAURUS
and ANGELO PETRAGLIA

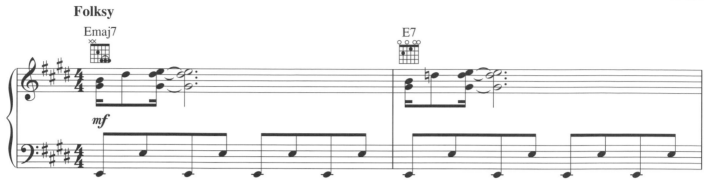

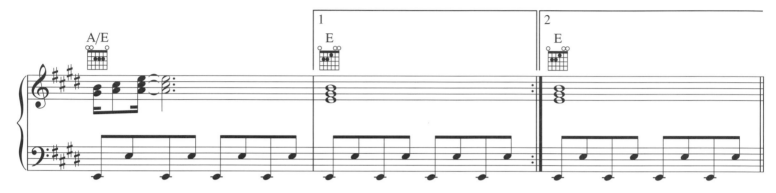

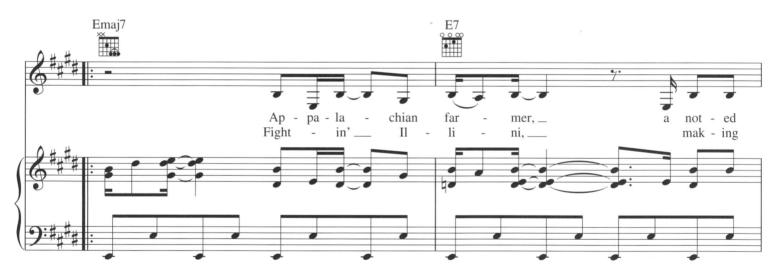

Ap- pa- la- chian far- mer, _____ a not- ed
Fight- in' _____ Il- li- ni, _____ mak- ing

charm- er _____ for- got the _____ field.
me cry _____ in a corn- field.

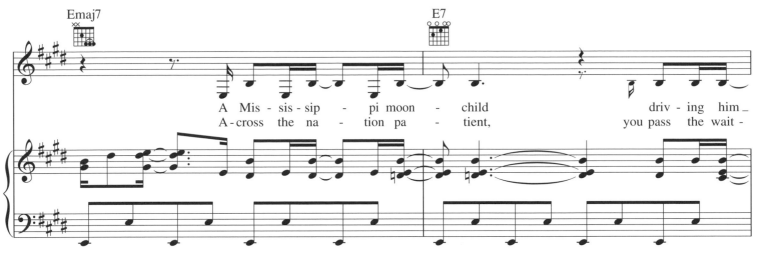

A Mis - sis - sip - pi moon - child   driv - ing him _
A - cross the na - tion pa - tient,   you pass the wait -

_ wild,   for - got to _ yield. _____
- ing   with a warm _ meal. _____

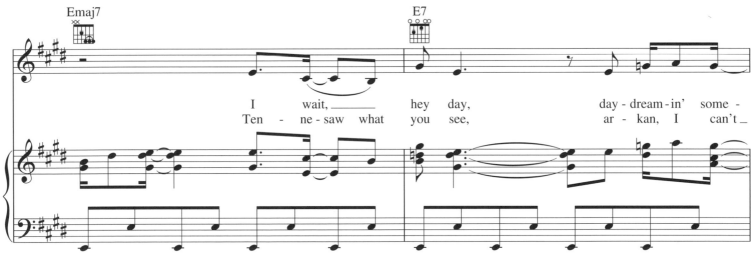

I wait, _____ hey day,   day - dream - in' some -
Ten - ne - saw what you see,   ar - kan, I can't _

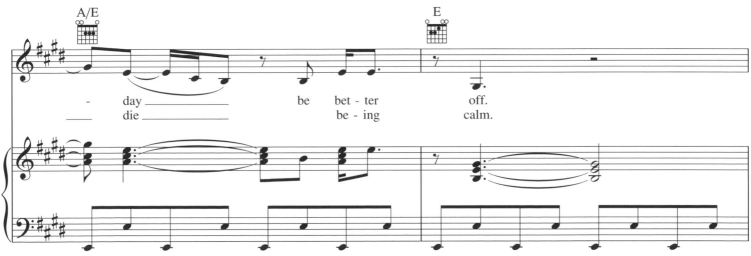

- day _____ be bet - ter   off.
_ die _____ be - ing   calm.

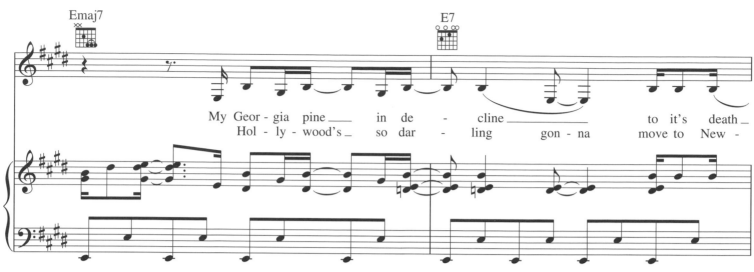

My Geor - gia pine ___ in de - cline ___ to it's death ___
Hol - ly - wood's ___ so dar - ling gon - na move to New -

'leans,
in a Flo - ri - da ___ swamp. ___
bet - ter sing a ___ song. ___

I've got a lot of love in,
I've got a lot of love in,

I've got a lot of love in my heart. ___

I'm gon-na get to heav-en,

I'm gon-na get to heav-en, ___
I'm gon-na count to sev-en, ___

I'm gon-na get to heav-en al-right. ___

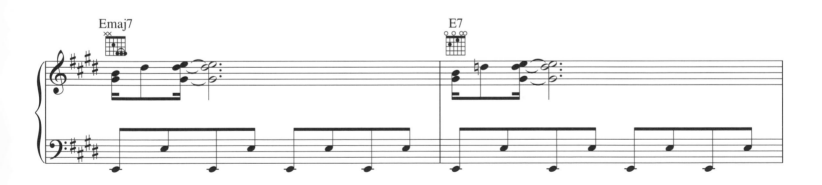

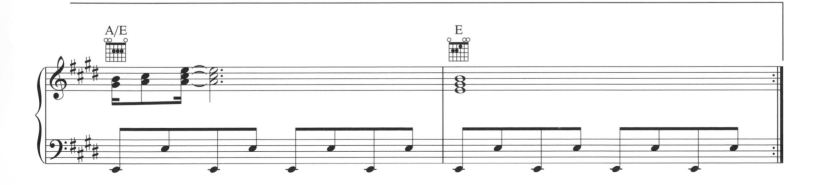

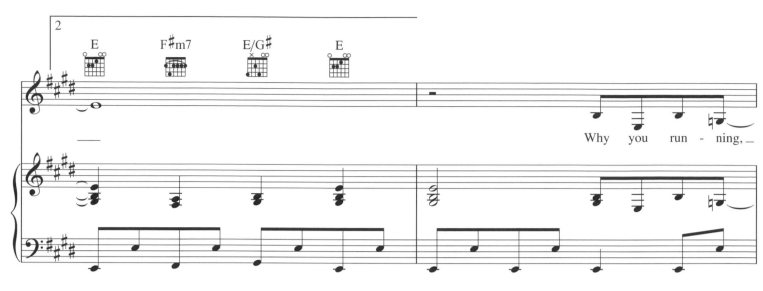

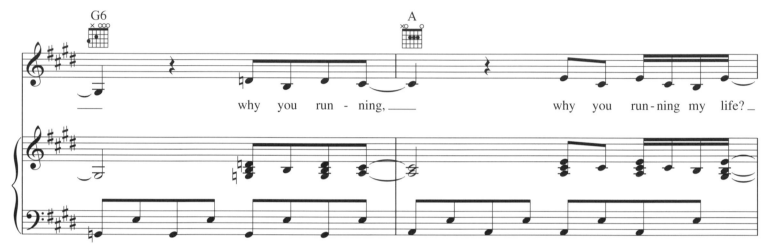

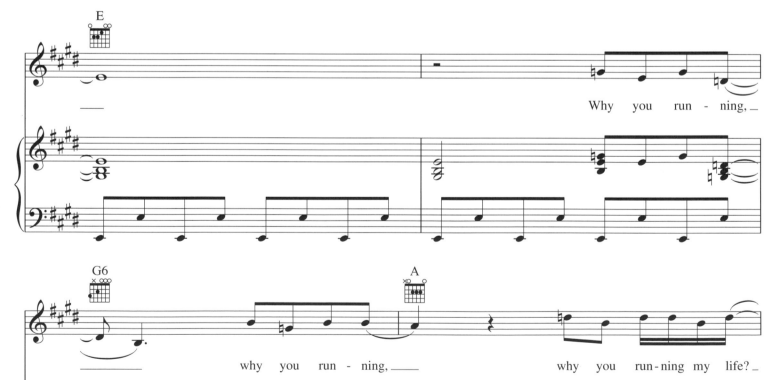

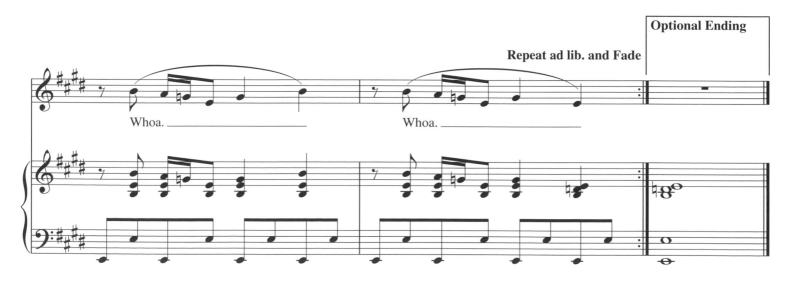

HOLDING OUT FOR A HERO

Words by DEAN PITCHFORD
Music by JIM STEINMAN

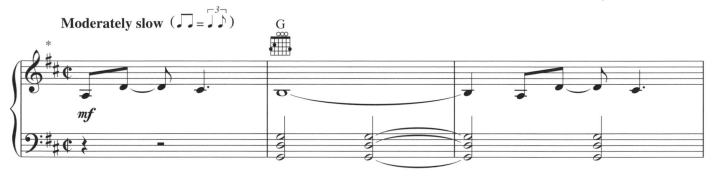

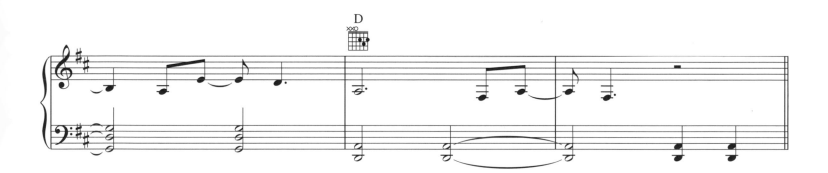

Where have all the good ___ men gone ___ and where ___ are the gods?
Some-where af - ter mid - night in ___ my wild - est fan - ta - sies, ___

Recorded a half step lower.

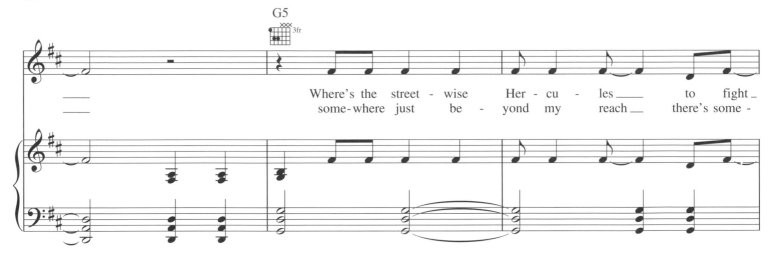

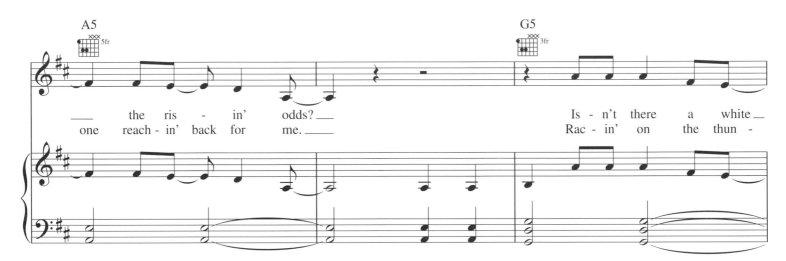

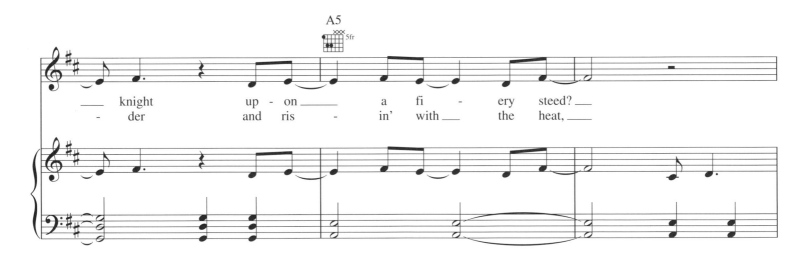

He's got - ta be sure, it's got - ta be soon _____ and he's got -
night. He's got - ta be strong, he's got - ta be fast _____ and he's got -

- ta be larg - er than life. _____ Larg - er than
- ta be fresh from the fight. _____

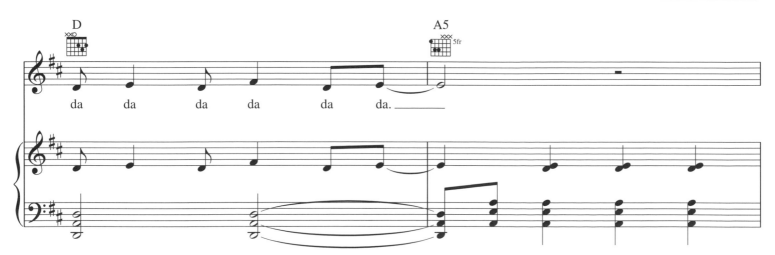

life.
(Da da da da da da _____ da da da

da da da da da da. _____

me. _____ Through the wind ___ and the chill and the rain ___

and the storm and the rag - in' flood, _ oh, his ___ ap - proach ___

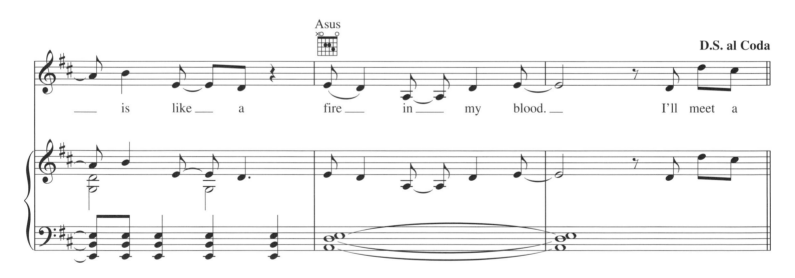

D.S. al Coda

___ is like ___ a fire ___ in ___ my blood. ___ I'll meet a

CODA

___ I need a he - ro. _____

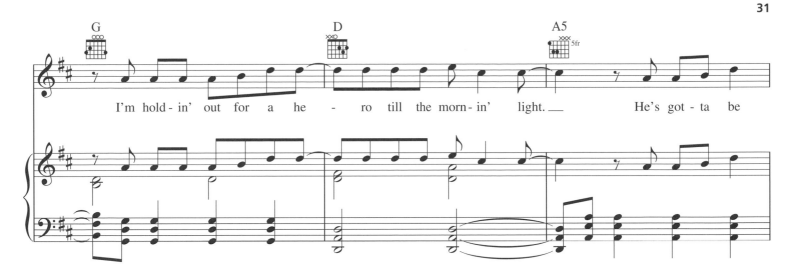

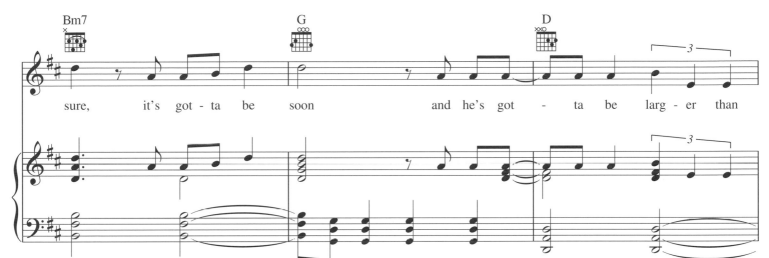

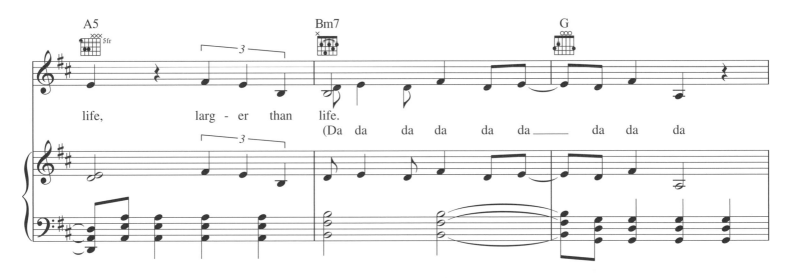

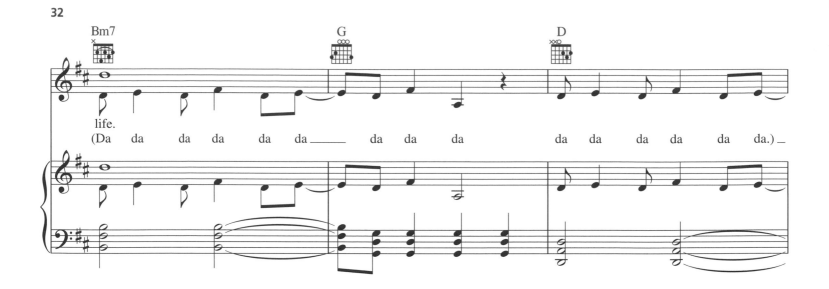

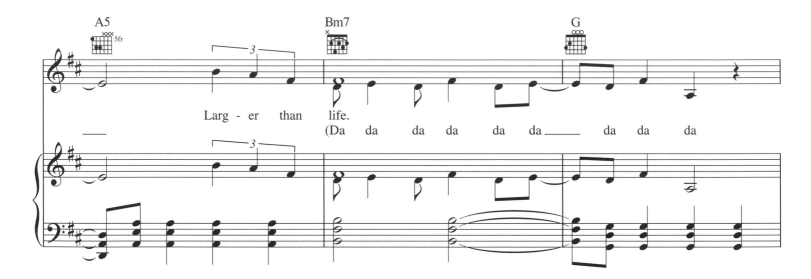

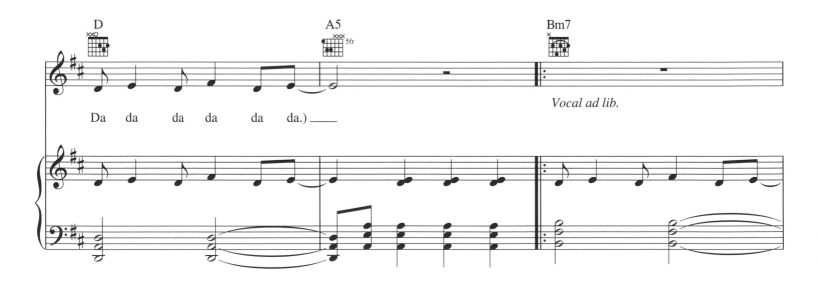

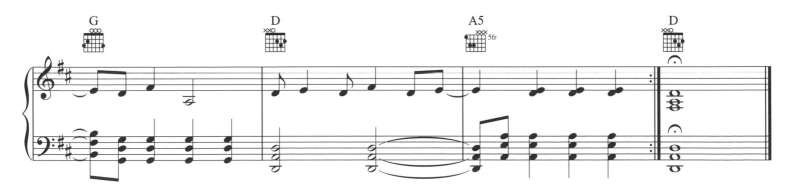

LET'S HEAR IT FOR THE BOY

Words by DEAN PITCHFORD
Music by TOM SNOW

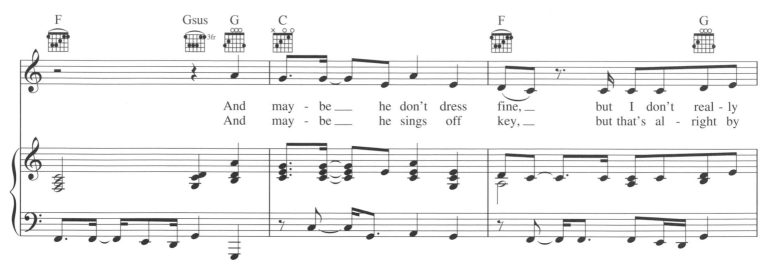

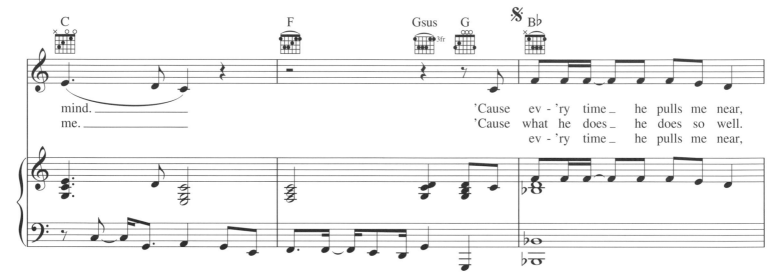

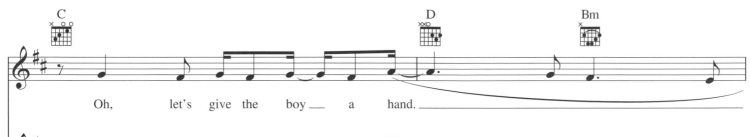

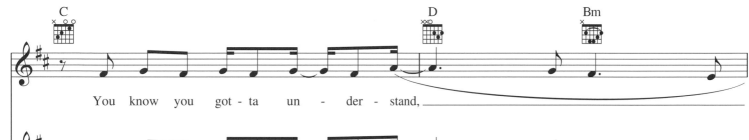

Let's hear it for ___ my ba - by.

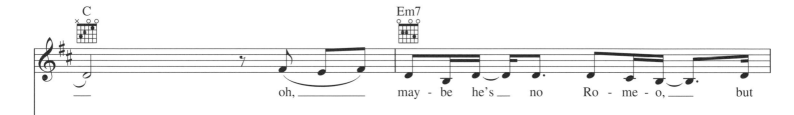

You know you got - ta un - der - stand, ___

oh, ___ may - be he's ___ no Ro - me - o, ___ but

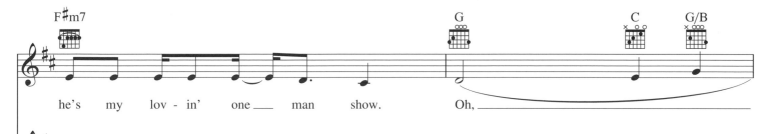

he's my lov - in' one ___ man show. Oh, ___

let's hear it for the boy! __

My

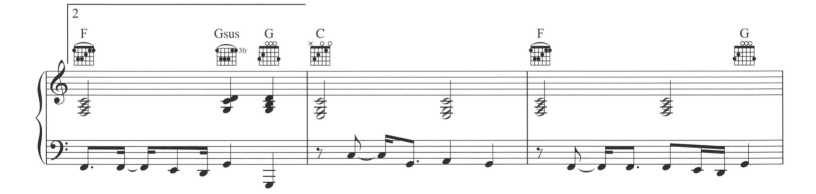

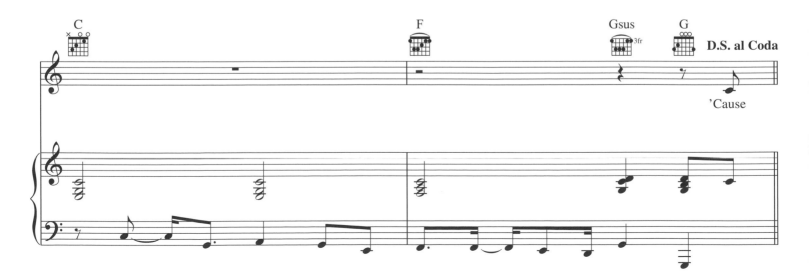

'Cause

SO SORRY MAMA

Words and Music by JOHN SHANKS,
WHITNEY DUNCAN and GORDIE SAMPSON

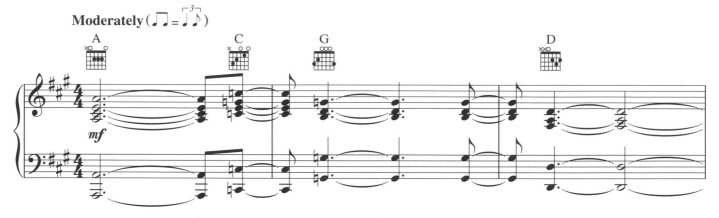

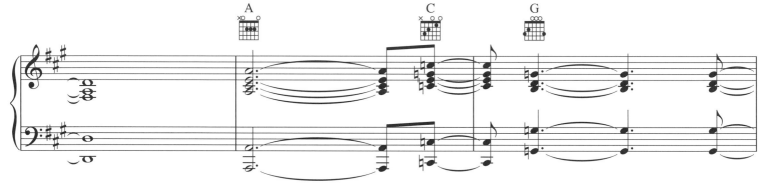

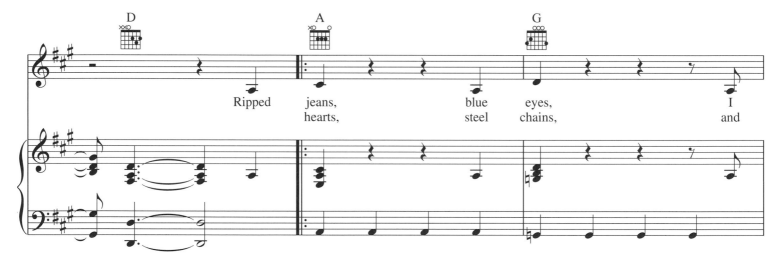

Ripped jeans, blue steel hearts, eyes chains, I and

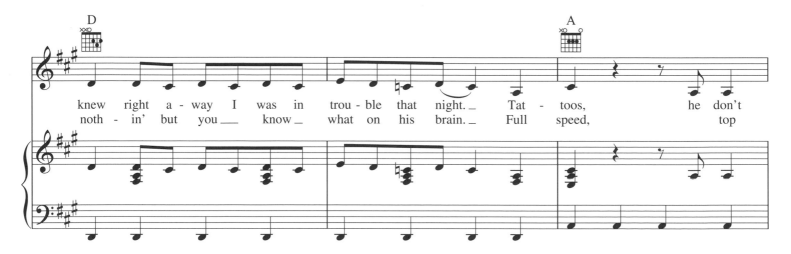

knew right a-way I was in trou-ble that night. Tat-toos, he don't
noth-in' but you know what on his brain. Full speed, top

I went __ wrong. I'm sor - ry, __ Ma - ma, so sor - ry, Ma - ma.

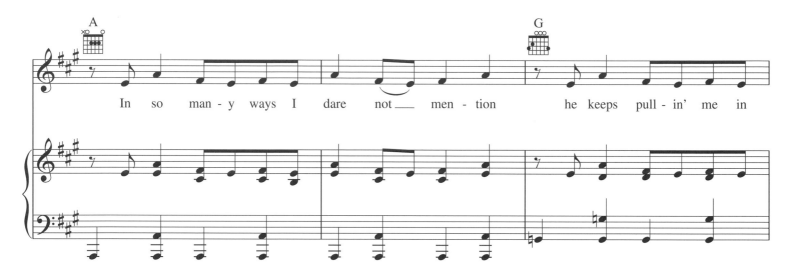

In so man - y ways I dare not __ men - tion he keeps pull - in' me in

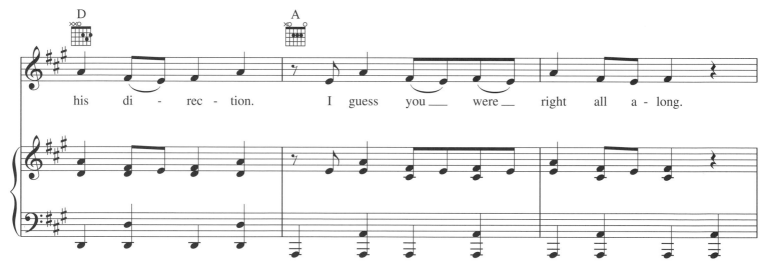

his di - rec - tion. I guess you __ were __ right all a - long.

So sor - ry, Ma - ma, so sor - ry, Ma - ma.

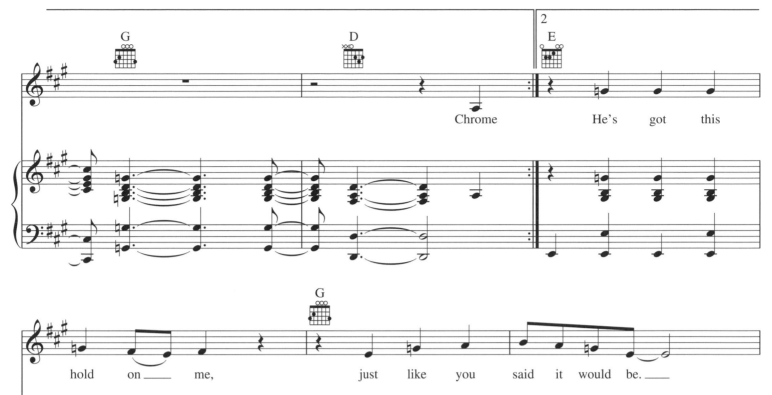

Chrome ____ He's got this

hold on ____ me, ____ just like you said it would be. ____

I did-n't miss him and now I can't walk a - way. ____

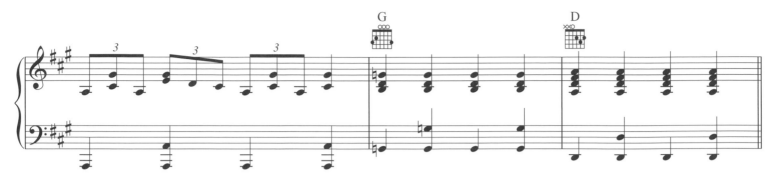

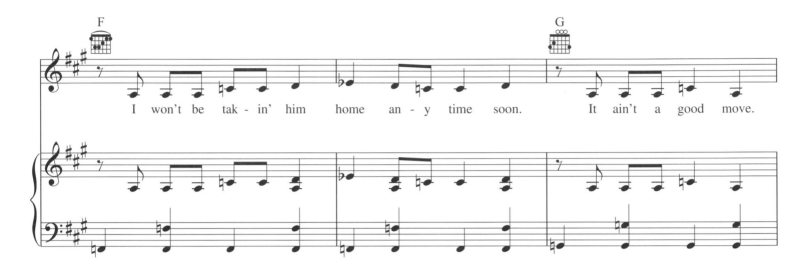

I won't be tak-in' him home an-y time soon. It ain't a good move.

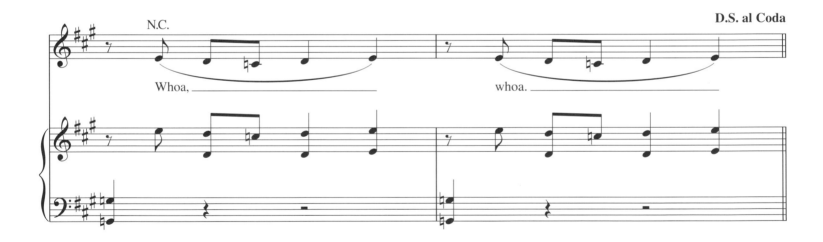

D.S. al Coda

Whoa, _____ whoa. _____

CODA

I'm sor-ry, Ma-ma, so sor-ry, Ma-ma.

(Na na___ na na, na na___ na.) I'm sor-ry,___ Ma - ma,

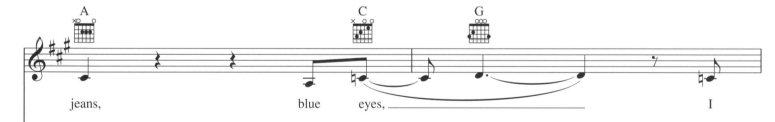

so sor-ry, Ma - ma. (Na na___ na na, na na___ na.) Ripped

jeans, blue eyes,_____ I

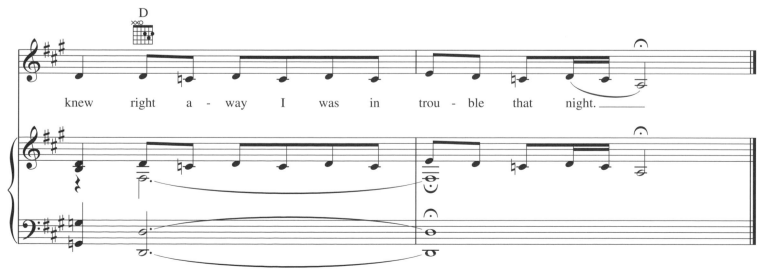

knew right a-way I was in trou-ble that night.___

FAKE ID

Words and Music by JOHN RICH
and JOHN SHANKS

Moderately fast

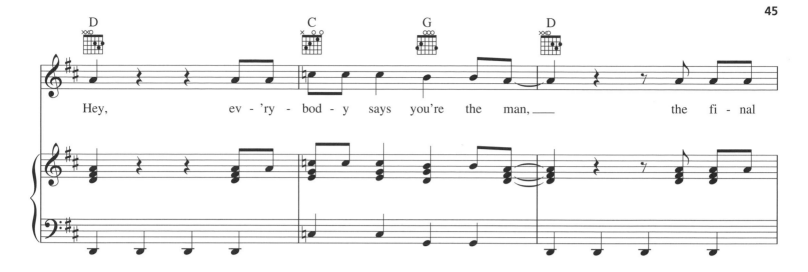

Hey, ev-'ry-bod-y says you're the man, ___ the fi - nal

piece to my mas - ter plan. ___ You got my world in the palm of your hand. ___

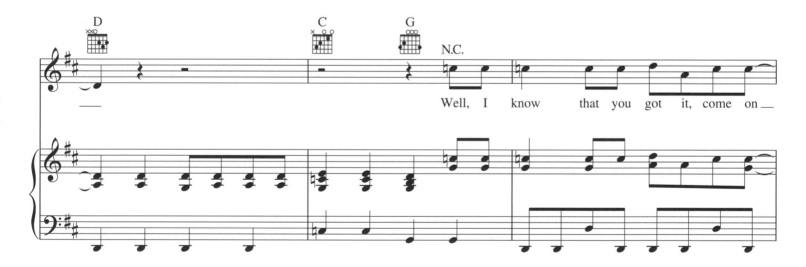

Well, I know that you got it, come on ___

___ and just sell it. Got the cash up in my pock - et, you know ___ I got - ta get it.

Hey, mis-ter, won't you sell me a fake __ I D? __

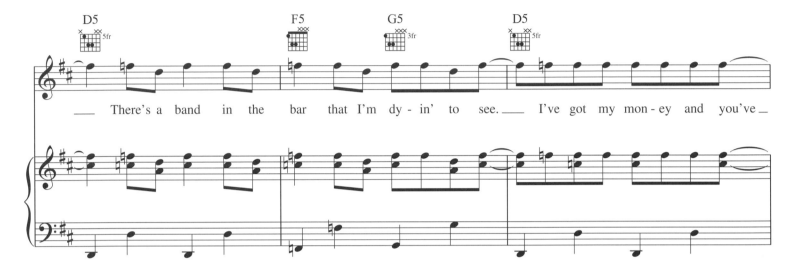

__ There's a band in the bar that I'm dy-in' to see. __ I've got my mon-ey and you've __

__ got what __ I need. __ Hey, mis-ter, won't you sell me a fake __ I D? __

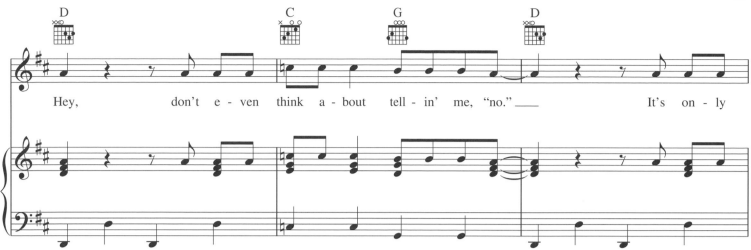

Hey, don't e-ven think a-bout tell-in' me, "no." ___ It's on-ly

twen-ty min-utes till the show. ___ Hey, ___ mis-ter, turn it o-ver, let's

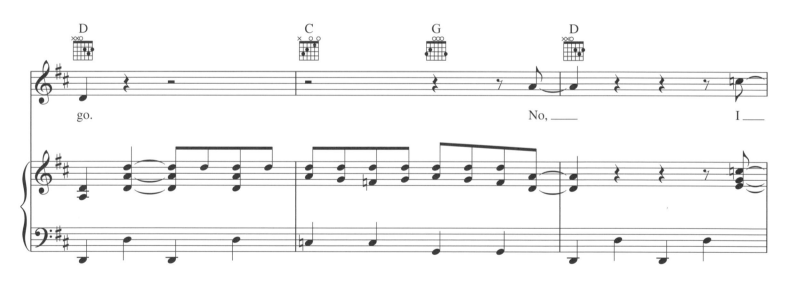

go. No, ___ I ___

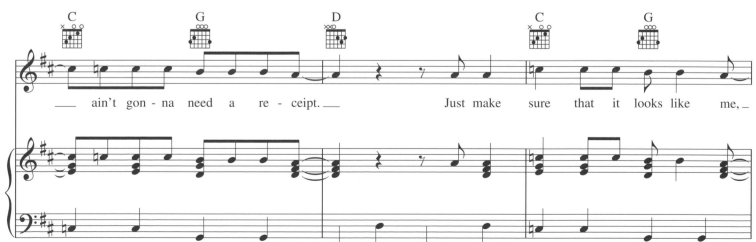

___ ain't gon-na need a re-ceipt. ___ Just make sure that it looks like me, ___

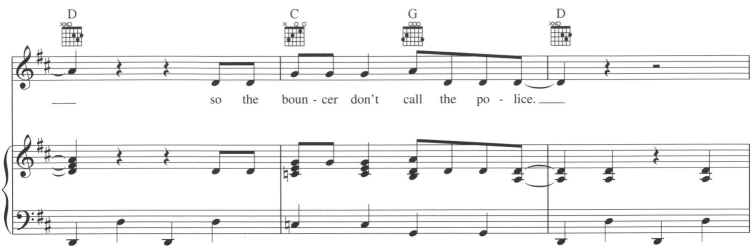

so the boun-cer don't call the po - lice. ___

N.C.

And don't tell my dad-dy, stole the keys to his Cad-die, don't dil-ly

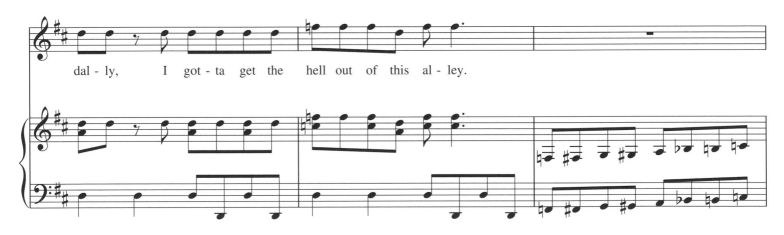

dal - ly, I got-ta get the hell out of this al - ley.

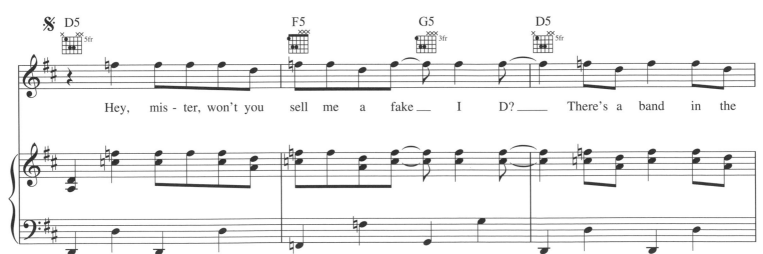

Hey, mis-ter, won't you sell me a fake ___ I D? ___ There's a band in the

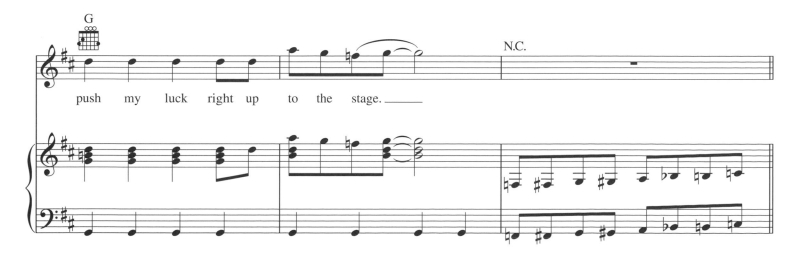

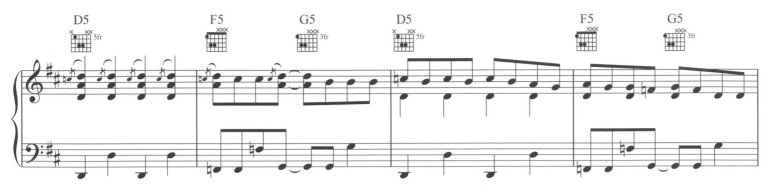

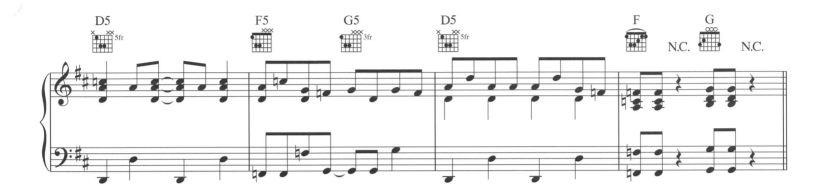

Hey, mis - ter, won't you sell me a fake __ I D? __ There's a band in the

bar that I'm dy - in' to see. __ I've got my mon - ey and you've __ got what __ I need. __

ALMOST PARADISE

Words by DEAN PITCHFORD
Music by ERIC CARMEN

Ballad

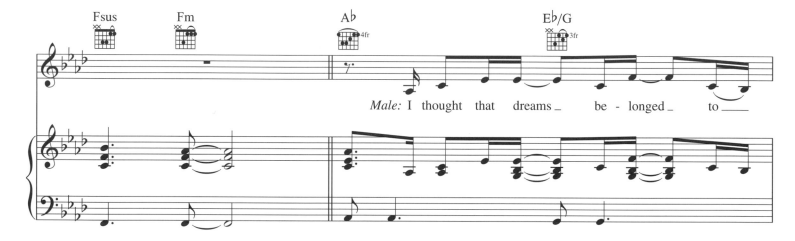

Male: I thought that dreams _ be - longed _ to _ oth - er men 'cause each time I ___ got close, _ they'd

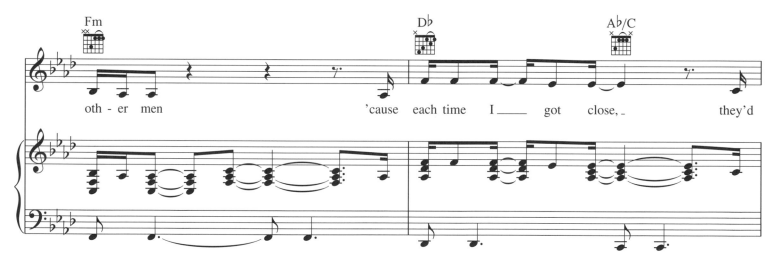

fall ___ a - part ___ a - gain. ___ Female: I feared my heart _ would beat _ in

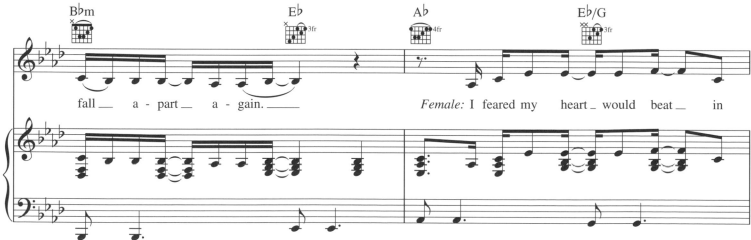

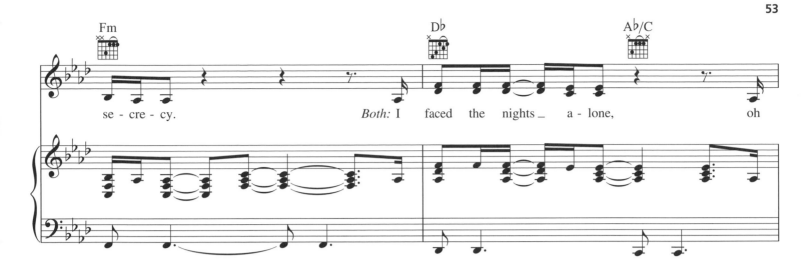

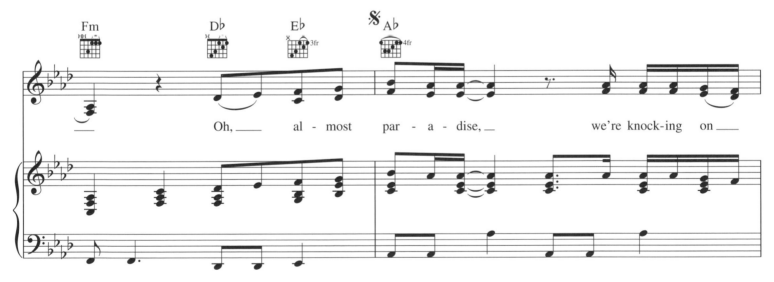

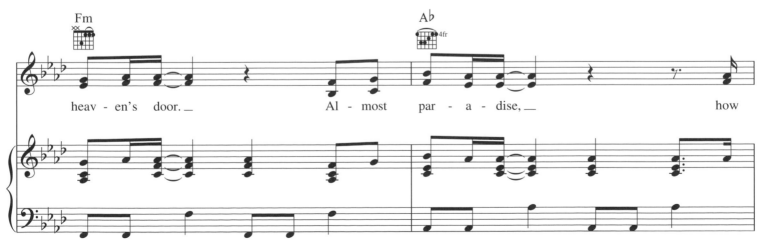

could we ask ___ for _____ more? I swear that I ___ can see for-ev-er

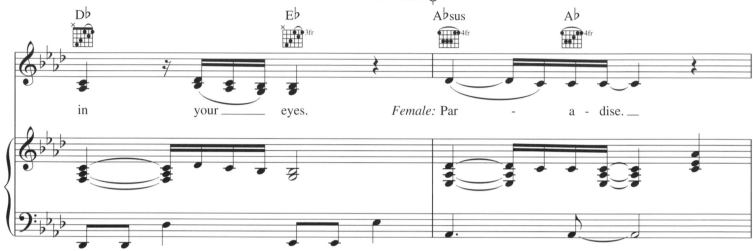

in your _____ eyes. *Female:* Par - a - dise. __

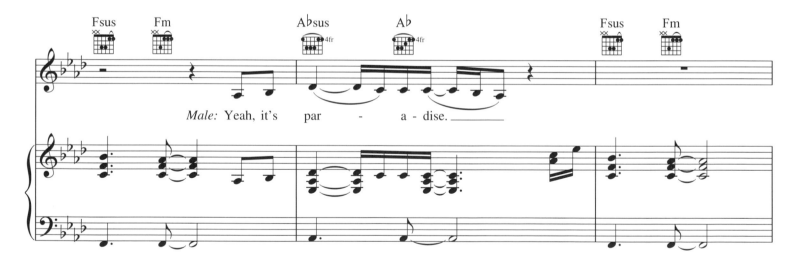

Male: Yeah, it's par - a - dise. _____

Female: It seems like per - fect love's __ so hard to find. I'd

al - most giv - en up, _____ you must have read ____ my ____ mind. _____

Both: And all these dreams _ I saved _ for a rain - y day. They're

fi - n'lly com - ing true, ____ you know I'll share them all ____ with you ____ 'cause

D.S. al Coda

now we hold ____ the fu - ture in ____ our hands. ____ Oh, ____ al - most

CODA

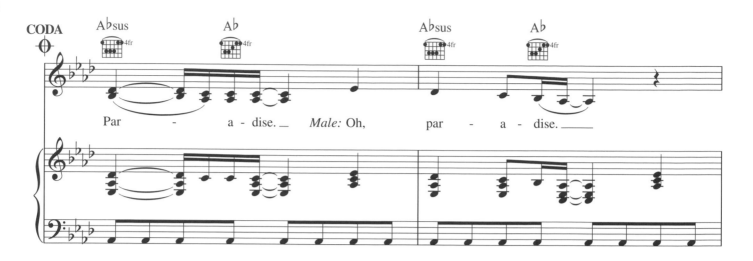

Par - a - dise. _ *Male:* Oh, par - a - dise. _

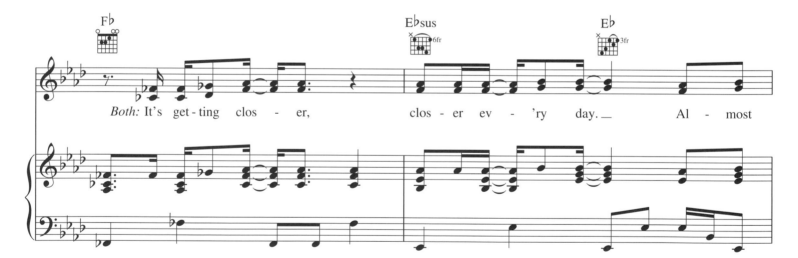

Female: And in your arms, _ sal - va - tion's not so far a - way. _

Both: It's get - ting clos - er, clos - er ev - 'ry day. _ Al - most

par - a - dise, _ we're knock - ing on _ heav - en's door. _ Al - most

par - a - dise, ___ how could we ask ___ for ___ more? I

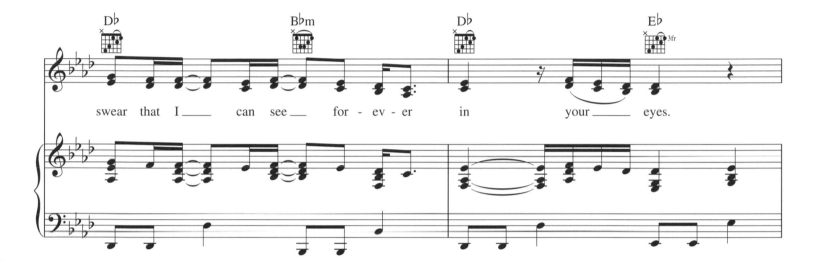

swear that I ___ can see ___ for - ev - er in ___ your ___ eyes.

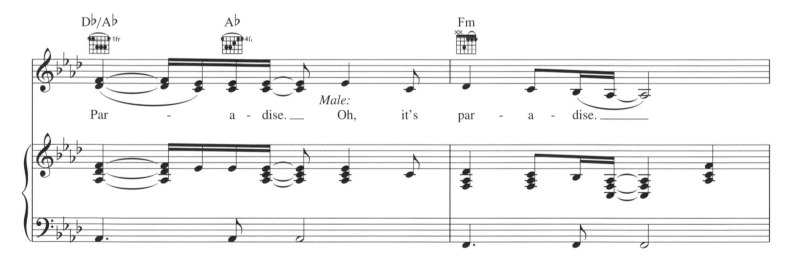

Male:
Par - a - dise. ___ Oh, it's par - a - dise. _____

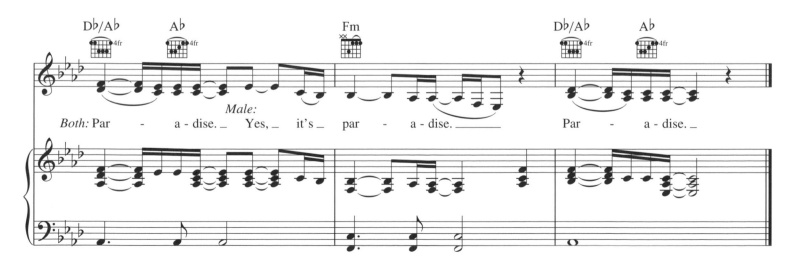

Both: Par - a - dise. _ *Male:* Yes, _ it's _ par - a - dise. _____ Par - a - dise. _

WALKIN' BLUES

Arranged by
R.L. BURNSIDE

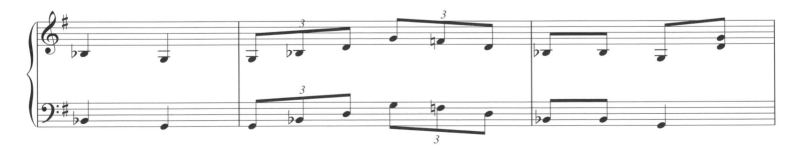

To Coda ⊕

D7

1. Well, I

2., 3. *(See additional lyrics)*

woke,   well, I woke up this morn-in' scram-blin'   for   my   shoe.

N.C.

That's all right, I had them old walk-in' blues. __

Additional Lyrics

2. Hey, what a good, what a good time
   You're tryin' to mine
   This ain't no mule train
   This ain't no friend of mine

3. Leave the mornin', I got to go
   I have to rob the blind
   But I been mistreated
   And I don't mind dying

MAGIC IN MY HOME

Words and Music by
JASON FREEMAN

SUICIDE EYES

Words and Music by JAREN JOHNSTON,
BILL SATCHER and MICHAEL HOBBY

Slow, driving Rock

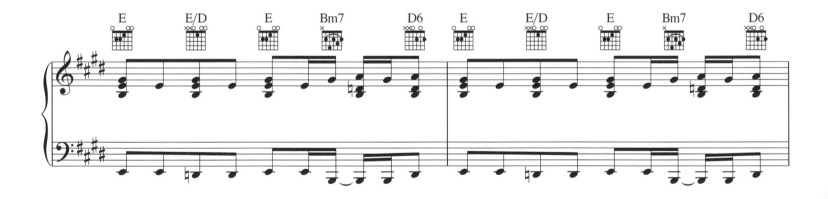

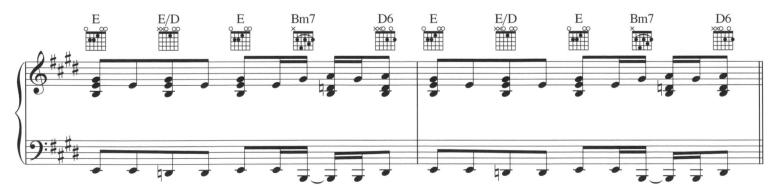

I on-ly seem to love the things that kill _____ me.

I on-ly seem to love the things that kill me. Take your

Take your

sticks and stones 'cause they don't break _ me, leave your guns at home, this ain't a west-ern, ba - by.

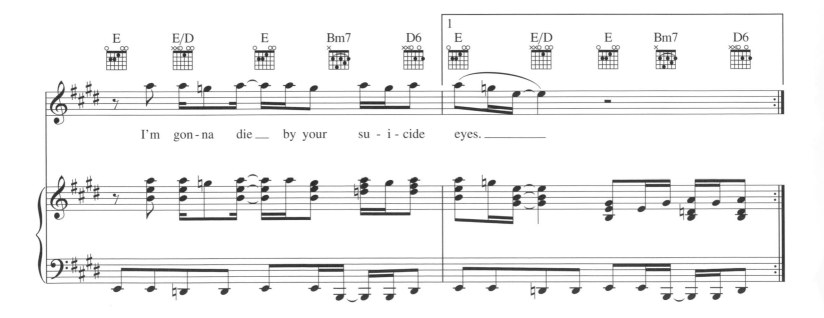

I'm gon-na die _ by your su - i - cide eyes. _____

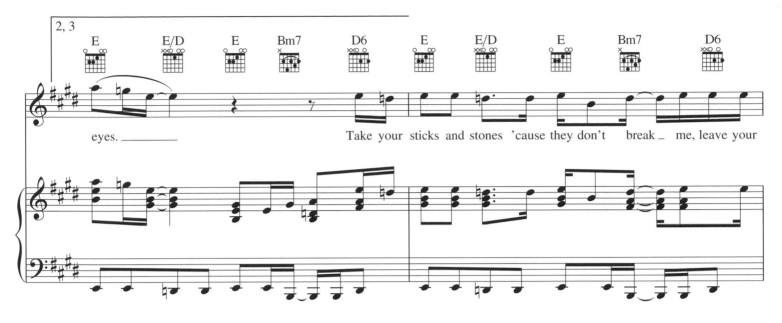

eyes. _____ Take your sticks and stones 'cause they don't break _ me, leave your

To Coda

guns at home, this ain't a west-ern, ba - by. I'm gon-na die __ by your su - i - cide

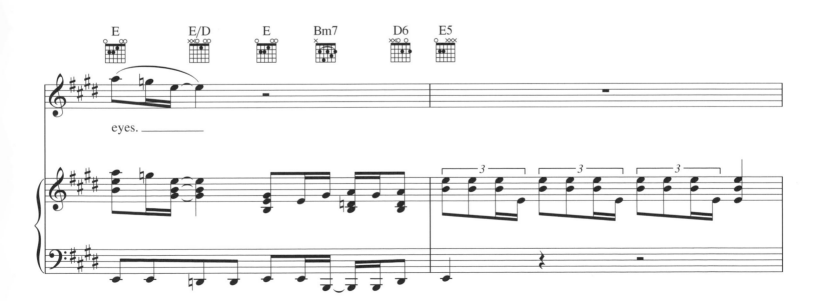

eyes. _____

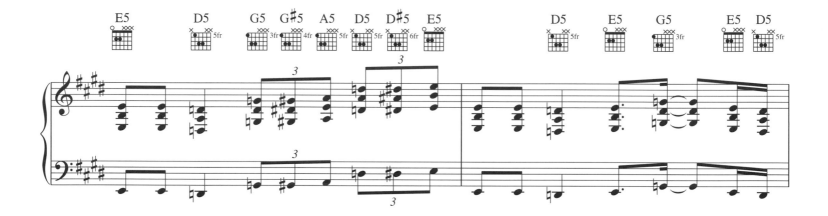

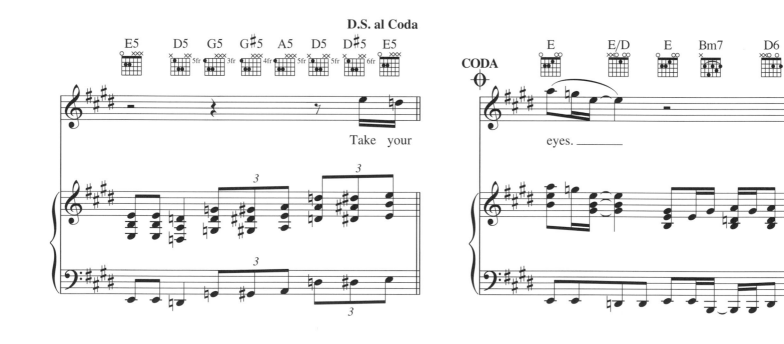

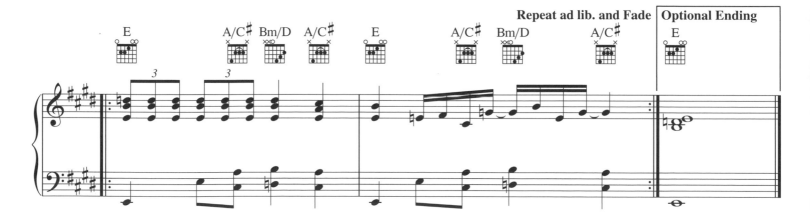

DANCE THE NIGHT AWAY

Words and Music by BILL WOLFER,
DEAN PITCHFORD, JAMES SMITH, LAVELLE W. CRUMP,
CHRISTOPHER GOODMAN and RASHIDA STAFFORD

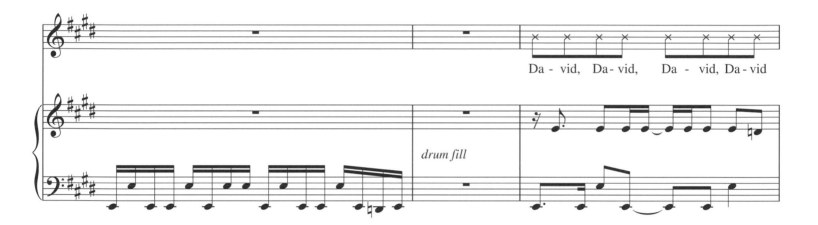

Da - vid, Da - vid, Da - vid, Da - vid Ban - ner, __ Ban - ner, Ban - ner.

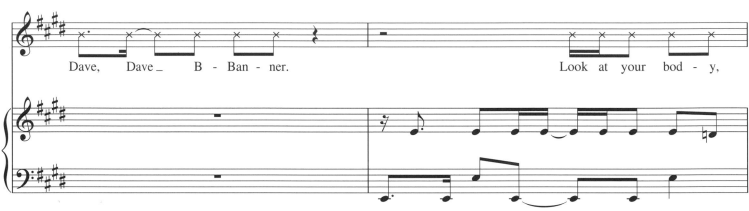

Dave, Dave __ B - Ban - ner. Look at your bod - y,

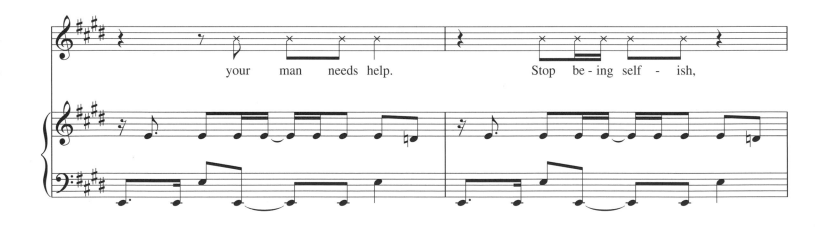

your man needs help. Stop be - ing self - ish,

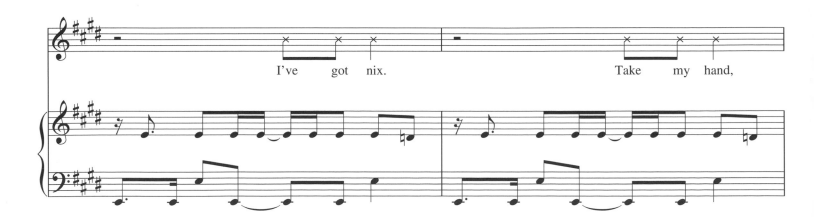

I've got nix. Take my hand,

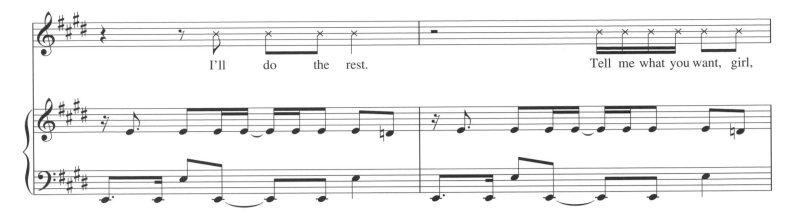

I'll do the rest. Tell me what you want, girl,

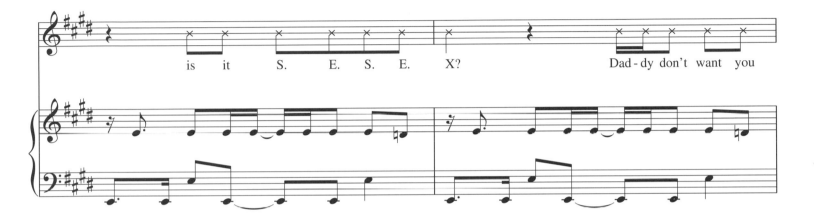

is it S. E. S. E. X? Dad-dy don't want you

hang-ing with a thug. I'll bet he's think-ing,

do we go... breathe real hard.

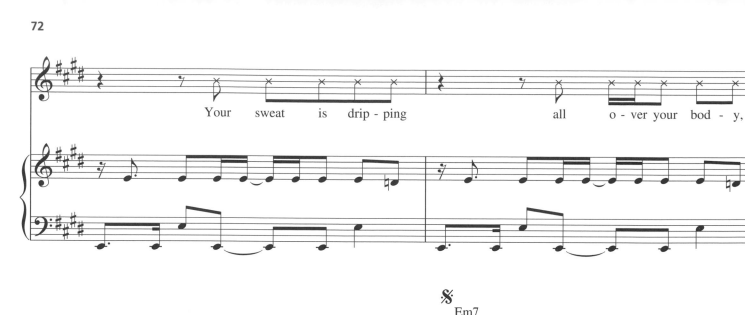

Your sweat is drip-ping all o-ver your bod-y,

let me give you what you're miss-ing. Grab your coat, grab your

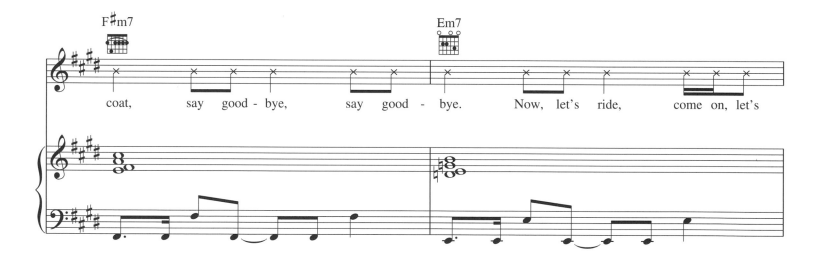

coat, say good-bye, say good-bye. Now, let's ride, come on, let's

ride. Now, let's ride, come on, let's ride. I feel the need, I feel the

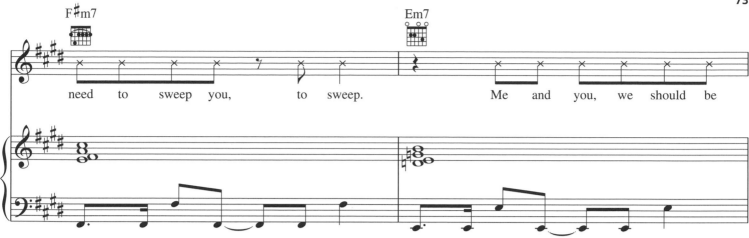

need to sweep you, to sweep. Me and you, we should be

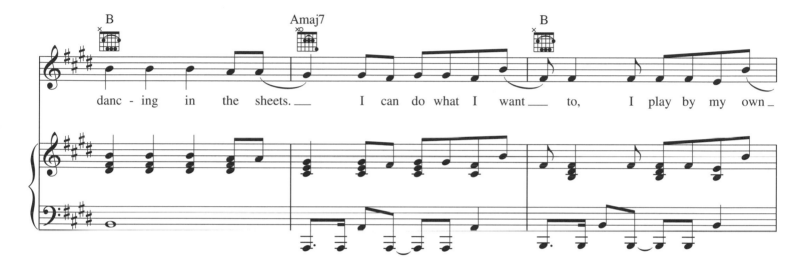

danc-ing in the sheets. I can do what I want to, I play by my own

rules. Come with me and let's just dance the night a-way. Don't wor-ry 'bout what I

do, watch me as I move on the floor and let's dance the night a-way.

It's my life and I ___ can be, like you, I can on - ly be ___ me.

Some call me a reb - el, you want to be him, let's go.

N.C.

D.S. al Coda

It's your life so don't ___ do you, don't let some - one con - trol ___ what you ___ do.

CODA

N.C.

E5

dance the night ___ a - way.

Oh no, I don't fol - low no rules.

But you'd

bet-ter keep tell-ing you what you've got to do. I do what-ev-er___ I want to.

Three four, let's go, hit the door. It's my life and I___ can be.

See, girl, come with D. B. Like you, I can on-ly be___ me.

Take my hand, girl, you can be free. Look in-to my eyes, girl, tell me what it is. We can

be at the club now, yeah, go-ing at it big. Or we can dance all night, you have a choice, let's live.

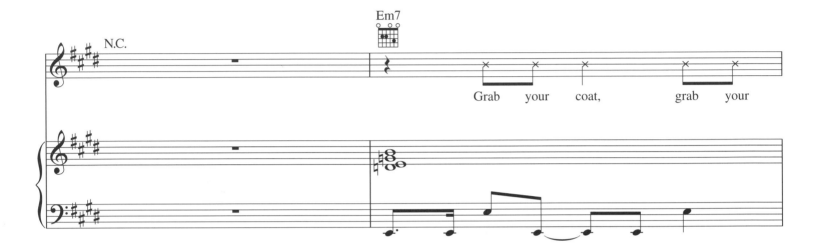

Grab your coat, grab your

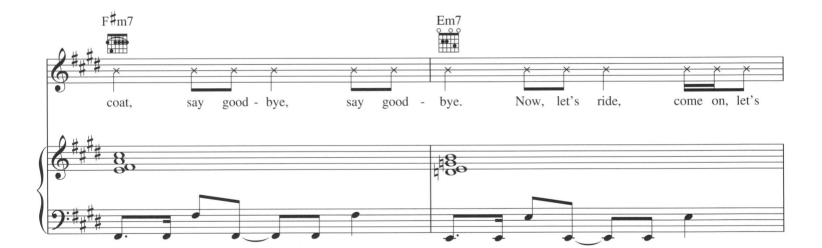

coat, say good-bye, say good-bye. Now, let's ride, come on, let's

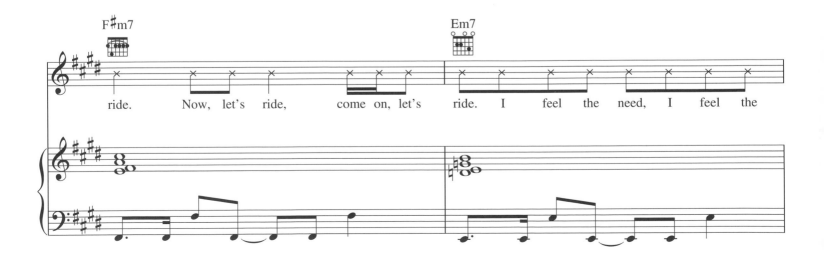

ride. Now, let's ride, come on, let's ride. I feel the need, I feel the

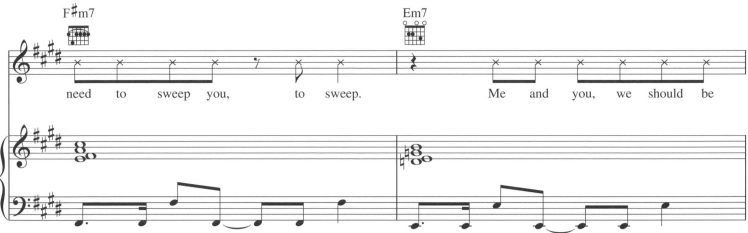

need to sweep you, to sweep. Me and you, we should be

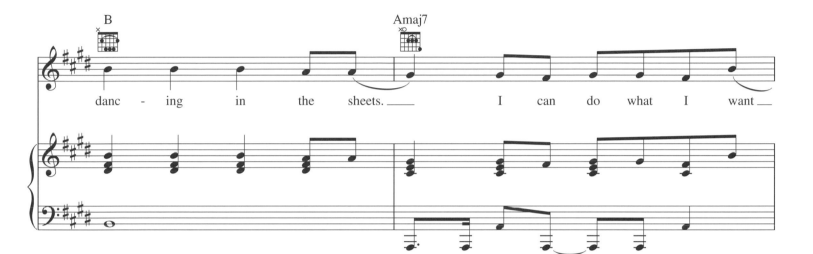

danc - ing in the sheets. ____ I can do what I want ____

____ to, I play by my own ____ rules. Come with me and let's just

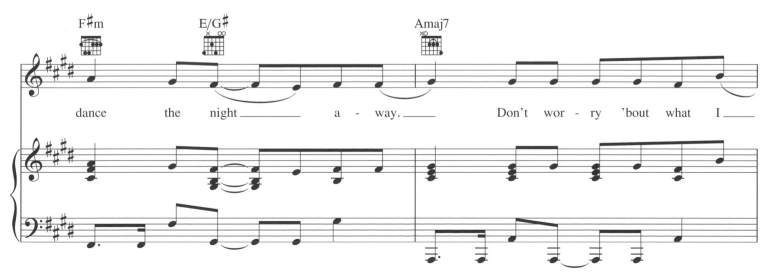

dance the night ____ a - way. ____ Don't wor - ry 'bout what I ____

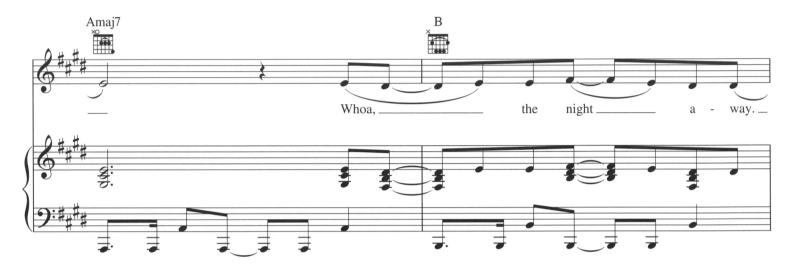